Central America
Facts and Figures

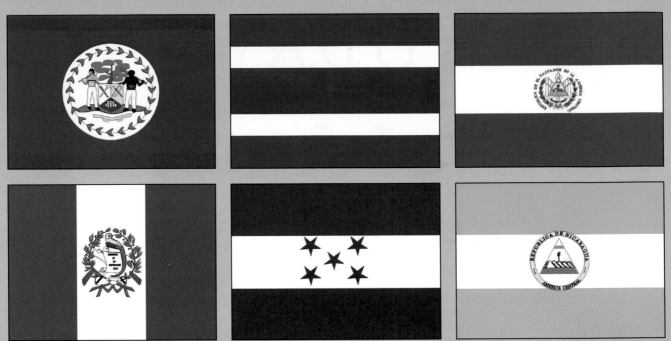

The Flags of Central America

Belize (top left): a royal blue flag with one horizontal red stripe at the top, one at the bottom, and a white circle with the coat of arms in the center. The motto *Sub Umbra Florero* on the coat of arms means, "Under the shade (of the mahogany tree) I flourish."

Costa Rica (top center): five horizontal bands of blue (top), white, red (double width), white, and blue.

El Salvador (top right): three horizontal bands of blue (top), white, and blue with the national coat of arms, which features a round emblem encircled by the words *Republica De El Salvador En La America Central*.

Guatemala (center left): a white vertical stripe between two blue vertical stripes with the coat of arms.

Honduras (center center): three equal horizontal bands of blue (top), white, and blue with five blue five-pointed stars arranged in an X pattern centered in the white band; the stars represent the members of the former Federal Republic of Central America: Costa Rica, El Salvador, Guatemala, Honduras, and Nicaragua.

Nicaragua (center right): three equal horizontal bands of blue (top), white, and blue with the national coat of arms centered in the white band; the coat of arms features a triangle encircled by the words *Republica De Nicaragua* on the top and *America Central* on the bottom.

Panama (bottom right): divided into four, equal rectangles; the top quadrants are white (hoist side) with a blue five-pointed star in the center and red; the bottom quadrants are blue (hoist side) and white with a red five-pointed star in the center.

CENTRAL AMERICA
TODAY

Central America
Facts and Figures

Charles J. Shields

Mason Crest Publishers
Philadelphia

Produced by OTTN Publishing, Stockton, N.J.

Mason Crest Publishers
370 Reed Road
Broomall PA 19008
www.masoncrest.com

Printed and bound in Malaysia.

First printing

1 3 5 7 9 8 6 4 2

Library of Congress Cataloging-in-Publication Data

Shields, Charles J., 1951-
  Central America : facts and figures / Charles J. Shields.
      p. cm. — (Central America today)
  Includes index.
  ISBN 978-1-4222-0645-4 (hardcover) — ISBN 978-1-4222-0712-3 (pbk.)
  1. Central America—Juvenile literature. I. Title.
  F1428.5.S55 2008
  972.8—dc22
                                              2008031992

CENTRAL AMERICA
TODAY

Belize   **Guatemala**
Central America: Facts and Figures   **Honduras**
Costa Rica   **Nicaragua**
El Salvador   **Panama**

Discovering Central America

James D. Henderson

CENTRAL AMERICA is a beautiful part of the world, filled with generous and friendly people. It is also a region steeped in history, one of the first areas of the New World explored by Christopher Columbus. Central America is both close to the United States and strategically important to it. For nearly a century ships of the U.S. and the world have made good use of the Panama Canal. And for longer than that breakfast tables have been graced by the bananas and other tropical fruits that Central America produces in abundance.

Central America is closer to North America and other peoples of the world with each passing day. Globalized trade brings the region's products to world markets as never before. And there is promise that trade agreements will soon unite all nations of the Americas in a great common market. Meanwhile improved road and air links make it easy for visitors to reach Middle America. Central America's tropical flora and fauna are ever more accessible to foreign visitors having an interest in eco-tourism. Other visitors are drawn to the region's dazzling Pacific Ocean beaches, jewel-like scenery, and bustling towns and cities. And everywhere Central America's wonderful and varied peoples are outgoing and welcoming to foreign visitors.

These eight books are intended to provide complete, up-to-date information on the five countries historians call Central America (Guatemala, El Salvador, Honduras, Nicaragua, Costa Rica), as well as on Panama (technically part of South America) and Belize (technically part of North America). Each volume contains chapters on the land, history, economy, people, and cultures of the countries treated. And each country study is written in an engaging style, employing a vocabulary appropriate to young students.

These colonial-style houses are a reminder of three centuries of Spanish rule.

All volumes contain colorful illustrations, maps, and up-to-date boxed information of a statistical character, and each is accompanied by a chronology, a glossary, a bibliography, selected Internet resources, and an index. Students and teachers alike will welcome the many suggestions for individual and class projects and reports contained in each country study, and they will want to prepare the tasty traditional dishes described in each volume's recipe section.

This eight-book series is a timely and useful addition to the literature on Central America. It is designed not just to inform, but also to engage school-aged readers with this important and fascinating part of the Americas.

Let me introduce this series as author Charles J. Shields begins each volume: *¡Hola!* You are discovering Central America!

(Opposite) A large cargo ship passes through the Panama Canal, an important waterway through Central America built in the early 20th century. (Right) One of many small islands, called cayes, off the coast of Belize. Central America is a tropical region with a diverse range of plants and animals. However, it is also facing an environmental crisis.

1 The Narrow Bridge of Land

CENTRAL AMERICA IS an *isthmus* joining North America to South America. In Panama, where the Panama Canal links the Caribbean Sea to the Pacific Ocean, the land at its narrowest point is only 30 miles (50 kilometers) wide. Central America borders Mexico on the north and Colombia on the south. With a total area of 202,000 square miles (523,000 square kilometers), Central America is about one-quarter the size of Mexico. Its wider western half is occupied by the nations of Belize, Guatemala, El Salvador, Honduras, and Nicaragua. The republics of Costa Rica and Panama occupy the narrower eastern half.

The terrain of Central America rivals many parts of the world for variety. Mountain peaks soar over 14,000 feet high in places. Dense, largely unexplored rainforests provide shelter not only for tens of thousands of species of plants, animals, and insects, but also for small tribes of Amerindians who have lived in

9

them for centuries. There are also deserts, plains, vast *pine barrens*, and high-altitude hardwood forests that resemble those in northern Europe.

Because of its narrowness, Central America is especially sensitive to movements of the Earth's crust. Far beneath the ground, gigantic *tectonic* plates barge into one another, triggering earthquakes and occasionally volcanic eruptions. Practically the entire region is an active earthquake zone. Since 1970, earthquakes in Guatemala and Nicaragua have killed 35,000 persons and badly damaged the capital cities. An earthquake with a *magnitude* of 7.6 on the *Richter scale* struck El Salvador in January 2001, resulting in the deaths of more than 700 people. A 6.1-magnitude earthquake the following month killed an additional 250 people. In fact, a major earthquake occurs somewhere in Central America almost every year.

Mountains and Volcanoes

The overwhelming geographic feature of Central America is its long, unbroken chain of mountains running north to south. The mountains of northern Central America are an extension of the mountain system of western North

Pacaya, a volcano in Guatemala, emits steam and ash. Central America is home to many active volcanoes. The volcanoes in the countries on the western coast of Central America are considered part of the "ring of fire," a circle of active volcanoes around the Pacific rim.

America. The ranges of southern Central America are *outliers* of the Andes Mountains of South America. Rugged mountains also crisscross the region, making transportation, communication, and economic development difficult. Nearly every country in Central America has a mountain range poking up against the sky.

The earthquakes and mountains of Central America go hand-in-hand with a third major characteristic of the region—volcanoes. Because the mountains of Central America are young, more than 20 of them are active. A mighty row of geologically recent volcanoes runs along Central America's Pacific shoreline. At 13,864 feet (4,210 m) high, Tajumulco, a volcano in Guatemala, is the region's highest peak.

As vents for *geothermal* energy, the volcanoes of Central America constantly threaten destruction. For example, El Salvador's Volcán Ilamatepec erupted in 2005, forcing over 2,000 people to flee their homes. On the other hand, Central America's famously fertile soil comes from the rich ash of volcanic eruptions. Most of Central America's 41 million people live within the volcanic regions and the narrow Pacific coastal plain that has been built up from eroding, older volcanoes. On the *mesetas*, or tablelands, between the mountains or on the cool, shady slopes themselves, the farmers and plantation owners of Central America grow bananas, coffee, and cotton.

Ridges, Valleys, and Plains

Mountains and volcanoes dominate the Pacific side of Central America, but the eastern Caribbean side rolls with ridges and valleys. Here, forces have compressed the Earth's crust, giving the rugged landscape a rumpled look. This area extends in an east-west arc across northwestern Central America. One edge follows the Caribbean shoreline of northern Honduras until it drops offshore to become the floor of the sea. Fewer people live in this part of Central America, but it contains greater mineral resources than the volcanic regions. Nicaragua exports gold, for example, and Honduras exports lead/zinc concentrates used in industry.

Low-lying plains are uncommon. Except for the narrow coastal strips along the Caribbean and Pacific shorelines, they are found only in northern Guatemala and the great Nicaraguan land depression that creates lakes Managua and Nicaragua. The lowlands offer the right kind of resources for cattle ranches and sugar cane plantations in Central America.

Climate: From Tropical to Cool

Although all of Central America is thought of as being tropical, its climate varies with altitude from tropical to cool. High up, the climate is cool, but down near the coast, there are steamy, tropical jungles, and the marshes of the Caribbean coast, including the aptly named Mosquito Coast, are especially hot and sticky. Four of Central America's seven capital cities are located in the cool uplands.

Rainfall varies a great deal. *Trade winds* passing over the warm waters of the Caribbean Sea produce heavy showers throughout the year on the eastern side of the region. In the interior and on the Pacific side, there is less rainfall. Most of it occurs during a wet summer season between May and October. Rainfall on the Pacific coastal plain is ideal for growing sugar cane and cotton. Year-round rainfall on the Caribbean plains feeds tropical rainforests and provides the right conditions for bananas.

Sudden, violent storms plague Central America. Hurricanes batter the Caribbean coast each summer and cause flooding, mudslides, and damage to roads and bridges.

The Environmental Challenge

Although Central America is home to an amazing range of exotic animals, such as jaguar, deer, puma, ocelot, armadillo, monkey, tapir, crocodile, and numerous species of reptiles and birds, the region faces a critical *biodiversity* challenge. Of the 11,046 plants and animals at risk of extinction in the world, 1,184 are in Central America and Mexico, where poverty and logging are shrinking habitats and wiping out species. Even Guatemala's national bird—a small, green creature with a red chest and long tail-feathers known as the quetzal—is at high risk, along with other lesser-known regional creatures, including the Pacific pilot whale.

Central America ranks among the world's poorest defenders of native plants and animals, despite most countries' efforts to create national parklands and preserves. Poverty that forces people to use cut-down forests for fuel and *poachers* who catch and sell rare animals for profit are a continuing threat. In addition, cash-strapped Central American governments often don't have the

A man offers an iguana for sale on the streets of Managua, Nicaragua. Most of the people living in Central America are poor, and some are willing to sell even endangered animals in order to make a living.

money to stop forest fires that rage out of control during dry seasons. Furthermore, the tremendous demand for beef in the United States has led to thousands of acres of rainforest being turned into pastureland for cattle raising.

In 2000, the United Nations Environment Program (UNEP), the World Bank, the U.S. Agency for International Development (USAID), and various other international and private organizations issued a joint report entitled "State of the Global Environment," warning that the environmental quality of Central America is rapidly getting worse.

(Opposite) Spanish cannons still overlook the harbor at Portobelo, Panama, from this stone fortress built during the 16th century. (Right) Nicaraguan Contra rebels stop near their camp on the border with Honduras. The Contras' guerrilla war against Nicaragua's Sandinista government was secretly financed by the United States government. The war in Nicaragua lasted through most of the 1980s, ending after a peace agreement was signed in 1987.

2 Central America's Troubled History

CENTRAL AMERICA'S HISTORY has been largely shaped by the ambitions of great powers. From the first arrival of the Spanish until now, Central America's modern history and identity has been tied to the importance of its location to other nations.

The Amerindian Past

Thousands of years before the first European contact with Central America, the ancestors of today's Central American Indians migrated to the region from the north. By about 400 B.C., the Maya Indians had become the most important culture of Central America.

Today, only hilltop ruins remain of the Mayan temples and towns that had begun to appear by A.D. 250. The ruins of Tikal in Guatemala, Copán in Honduras, and Tazumal in El Salvador are relics of that civilization. Panama and most of Costa Rica were home to less-developed societies, more like the Indians of northern South America at the time.

The Maya were highly skilled engineers, architects, and builders. They planned and constructed great cities; irrigated surrounding fields of corn, beans, and squash using a system of canals; and even charted the nighttime skies. Some of their history is preserved in their *hieroglyphic* writings.

However, the ancient Maya have also left our world a mystery to solve. Why did they begin to abandon their cities by about A.D. 900? Had they lost control of their empire? Did food shortages or disease bring about their decline as a power? Even though today their descendants live in the mountains of Mexico as well as in Central America—and still speak Mayan languages—the reasons for the collapse of the Mayan civilization are unclear.

By the time the first Europeans sighted Central America, its people had split into smaller groups. There were the Pipils in El Salvador, for example, who resembled the Aztecs of Mexico in some ways; the Quiché, Cakchiquel, and Mam peoples of Guatemala, related to the Maya; and the Chorotegas, or "Fleeing People," who had come to Costa Rica from southern Mexico in the 14th century.

The Coming of Europeans

In 1501, Rodrigo de Bastidas and Juan de la Cosa of Spain became the first Europeans to explore the Central American coast. In 1502, Italian explorer Christopher Columbus sailed the Caribbean shore from Honduras to Panama and claimed the land for Spain, whose king and queen had sponsored his voyage. Vasco Núñez de Balboa crossed Panama in 1513, establishing that the isthmus was the shortest way to the Pacific Ocean from the Caribbean.

Then, a wave of Spanish conquistadors (conquerors) came on the heels of the explorers, invading Central America and fighting the Indians throughout the region. During 1523–1525, Pedro de Alvarado defeated the Indians of Guatemala and El Salvador. Francisco Hernández de Córdoba founded the settlements of León and Granada, adding Nicaragua to the Spanish empire. In Honduras, the chief of the Lenca tribe, Lempira, led 30,000 Indians against the Spanish. However, he was betrayed and treacherously murdered at peace talks in 1538. Less than 50 years after claiming Central America, the Spanish had completed their conquest of it. By then, many Indians had been killed or sent as slaves to plantations in the West Indies.

In 1570, the Spanish established an administrative center, called an *audiencia*, in Guatemala. The Audiencia of Guatemala ruled over all of Central America except Panama. (Panama, at first part of the **Viceroyalty** of Peru, came under the control of the Viceroyalty of New Granada in 1718 and was ruled from Colombia.) The Audiencia of Guatemala itself was a subdivision of the Viceroyalty of New Spain, which governed most of the Spanish colonies in North America from its headquarters in Mexico City.

Central America remained under the banner of Spain for nearly three centuries. However, the Spanish rulers paid more attention to Mexico and Peru and their treasures of gold and silver. Central America had little wealth to export by comparison. In addition, Central America was more costly to defend than many people felt the colonies deserved.

A snake crawls out of the mouth of a Mayan rain god in a stone sculpture discovered at the Copán ruins in Honduras. Copán once was one of several centers of the Mayan civilization, which flourished throughout Central America from about 1000 B.C. to A.D. 900.

In 1638, for instance, a band of shipwrecked English sailors landed on the shore of Belize. Later, English Puritans established trading posts on the coast, just as fellow Puritans had already done in New England in North America. Over the next 100 years, more English settlements were established, although a rougher breed of settler gradually replaced the Puritans—English, Scottish, and Irish pirates mainly. In their ragtag ships they struck out at passing Spanish *galleons* loaded with gold, silver, and hardwoods. In 1798, while Spain and Britain were at war, a Spanish fleet roamed the coast, pounding villages with cannon-fire.

Meanwhile, over the years, missionaries from Spain established an educational system in Central America and converted the Indians to the Roman Catholic religion. Settlers developed a plantation system of raising bananas, sugar cane, and tobacco. Despite this, Central America remained an underdeveloped *backwater* of the Spanish empire.

Independence

In 1808, Napoleon I of France invaded Spain and forced the Spanish king into exile. As a result, Spain's grip on its colonies was weakened. On September 15, 1821, the Audiencia of Guatemala declared its independence, removing from Spanish control all of Central America except Panama. That same year, Panama broke away from Spanish rule and became a province of the newly independent nation of Colombia. The independence movement succeeded throughout Central America with little bloodshed.

What is now Belize had belonged to the Audiencia of Guatemala, too, but Spain had never brought the region under its control. In the mid-1800s, Britain took formal possession of the Belize area, making it a colony called British Honduras. Belize remained a British colony from 1862 until 1981, when it was granted independence as a British Commonwealth country, similar to Canada or Australia.

Attempts at Unification

Over the next 150 years, Central America tried 25 times to unify its countries into one nation. In 1822, for example, Costa Rica, El Salvador, Guatemala, Honduras, and Nicaragua became part of Mexico. In 1823, however, they broke away from Mexico and formed a political union called the United Provinces of Central America. Bitter rivalries caused this union to collapse in 1838. Each state had become an independent republic by 1841.

In 1842, El Salvador, Honduras, and Nicaragua created the Central American Confederation. This government proved too weak to enforce its rule, however, and it collapsed in 1845. In 1907, Costa Rica, El Salvador, Guatemala, Honduras, and Nicaragua created the Central American Court of Justice. This court handled cases between the nations. It was dissolved in 1918 after Nicaragua had ignored its findings in a dispute over canal-building rights. In 1921, El Salvador, Guatemala, and Honduras united under a central government called the Central American Federation. However, rivalries and disagreements among members caused the federation to collapse in less than a year.

Generally, Central America has had better luck at forming loose unions based on common interests. In 1948, all the Central American states except Belize joined with other Latin American countries and the United States to form the Organization of American States (OAS). This organization promotes cultural, economic, and political understanding among member nations. Belize joined the OAS in 1991.

In 1960, El Salvador, Guatemala, Honduras, and Nicaragua formed the Central American Common Market (CACM). Costa Rica joined in 1963. This organization provides for free trade among member nations. It created the Central American Bank for Economic Integration. This bank promotes economic cooperation and invests in industries needed to supply the area as a whole.

Foreign Powers Take an Interest

Independence from Spain in 1821 freed Central American countries to pursue their own interests, but it also exposed them to rivalries and, as small countries, to the designs of great world powers.

For the rest of the 19th century, the history of Central America was torn by internal conflicts between those who supported the traditions of Spain and the Catholic church and those who called for a union of the states of Central America. Added to this, foreign powers vied for control of the region. First, a passage across the isthmus of Panama was highly desirable among large nations for shipping. Second, Britain intended to maintain its influence along the Caribbean shoreline. Third, the United States began to exercise control over Central America under the Monroe Doctrine, which argued that the United States had a right to maintain the security of the Caribbean region.

After its victory over Spain in the Spanish-American War of 1898, the United States began to exert more and more influence over Central America. Three times between 1907 and 1924, the United States took a hand militarily in Honduras, and twice U.S. troops occupied Nicaragua, in 1912 and 1933, for similar reasons. Many times, at the center of U.S. concerns over Central America was its military and economic importance as the shortest way between the Atlantic and Pacific oceans.

The discovery of gold in California in 1848 fueled competition for exclusive rights to routes across Nicaragua and Panama. The British tried to cement their control of the Caribbean entrance to a canal across Nicaragua by occupying the port of San Juan del Norte between 1848 and 1850 and renaming it Greytown. In 1851, Cornelius Vanderbilt established a highly profitable route across Nicaragua by waterway and carriage road. A railroad under the control of the United States was completed across Panama in 1855.

However, the building of a trans-isthmian canal did not take place until the beginning of the 20th century. From 1880 to 1900, a French company under Ferdinand de Lesseps attempted unsuccessfully to construct a sea-level canal on the site of the present-day Panama Canal. In November 1903, with U.S. and French support, Panama proclaimed its independence from Colombia and concluded the Hay-Bunau Varilla Treaty with the United States.

The treaty granted rights to the United States to act freely in a zone roughly 10 miles wide and 50 miles long. In that zone, the U.S. would build a canal, then administer, fortify, and defend it for all time, according to the treaty. In 1914, the United States completed the existing 50-mile (83 km) lock canal, one of the world's greatest engineering triumphs. However, beginning in the 1960s, a *nationalist* movement inside Panama called for renegotiating the treaty with the United States.

Nationalism in Central America

After World War II, nationalistic movements in Central America grew rapidly. Led by intellectuals and military figures who resented Central America's role as a pawn in world affairs, they tended to call for the removal of foreign power in Central America and improvement in the economic and social welfare of the poor. Military governments in Guatemala and El Salvador were overthrown in 1944. Worker strikes in Honduras in 1954 forced the United Fruit Company, which owned many banana plantations, to reduce its economic control over plantations, railways, and ports. After riots in Panama in the early 1960s, the United States agreed to review its ownership of the Canal Zone.

Additional conflict resulted from disagreements among Central American nations. Border tensions, except between Costa Rica and Panama, were common throughout the region. This was particularly true along borders between El Salvador, Honduras, Nicaragua, and Costa Rica. Guatemala continued to pressure Belize for border adjustments.

Civil War

Much more serious, however, were armed political rebellions. In Guatemala, armed rebels, directed from Communist Cuba beginning in 1960, waged *guerrilla* war against the government, a conflict that would continue for 36 years. Four principal *left-wing* guerrilla groups targeted businesses and government buildings and fought government security forces.

During the 1970s, discontent in El Salvador with social problems, a poor economy, and the repressive dictatorship grew violent. By 1979, guerrilla warfare was widespread throughout the country. About 1 million Salvadorans—one-fifth of the population—fled to neighboring Central American countries and the United States. Hundreds of thousands more sought safety by crowding into El Salvador's cities. Both the guerrillas and the poorly trained Salvadoran armed forces terrorized the population with random killings. The United States, believing the best hope for peace lay with the government, sided with the Salvadoran military.

In 1979, anti-government guerrilla forces under the leadership of the Sandinista National Liberation Front (FSLN) overthrew the U.S.–backed government. Although the Sandinistas pledged to remain neutral in Central American politics, American president Ronald Reagan accused them of supplying arms to Communist rebels in El Salvador with the aid of Cuba and the Soviet Union. The Reagan administration stepped up its opposition to the Sandinista government by aiding a resistance movement called the Contras to overthrow the Sandinistas. Most of the Contra forces operated out of Honduras.

The war between the Sandinistas and the Contras intensified from 1985 to 1987, with members of the United States Congress accusing the Reagan administration of secretly supplying arms and money to the Contras without approval. Because the Contras were funded with money received by the secret sale of weapons to Iran, the issue became known as the Iran-Contra Affair.

In response to nearby civil wars in Central America, Costa Rica issued a proclamation of neutrality in 1983. In 1986, Costa Ricans elected as their president a young sociologist and lawyer, Oscar Arias Sánchez. As a result of his efforts, five Central American presidents signed his peace plan in Guatemala City in 1987, for which he received the Nobel Peace Prize that year. In all, the Central American civil wars of 1970–1996 resulted in the deaths of 300,000 people.

The Issue of the Isthmus Again

International attention again returned to the strategic importance of the Panama Canal on December 20, 1989, when the United States invaded Panama to oust the country's dictator, General Manuel Antonio Noriega, whom they accused of drug trafficking. The United States' goal was to install a friendly government. However, the Organization of American States and the United Nations passed resolutions condemning the invasion.

Oscar Arias Sánchez, the president of Costa Rica from 1986 to 1990, won the 1987 Nobel Peace Prize for his program for peace in Central America. His Costa Rican presidential term will be in effect until 2010.

Under new treaties, the United States was responsible for operating and defending the Panama Canal until December 31, 1999. Since that date, the United States and Panama have together maintained the Canal's neutrality. Merchant and naval vessels of all nations have access to the Canal and pay tolls. However, the United States continues to have the obligation of ensuring that the Canal remains open and secure. The day-to-day responsibility for managing the Canal has completely passed into the hands of Panama.

(Opposite) A Nicaraguan woman picks cotton, a crop introduced to Central America during the 1950s. (Right) A Panamanian worker throws a bunch of bananas into the back of his pickup truck. Historically, bananas have been one of the region's major export crops for more than a century. Many of the people of Central America work the land, growing food for themselves. Others labor in small factories and plantations.

3 Struggling Economies Face Serious Challenges

THE PEOPLE OF Central America are among the world's poorest. Much of the land still belongs to a rich few. A great deal of land is also devoted to growing "cash crops"—crops that can be sold abroad, like coffee and sugar—rather than food for local people. In 2000, the Central American nations, with a combined population of around 36 million and economic output of $67 billion, accounted for only 0.2 percent of the world's economic activity.

Banana and Coffee Republics

As a Spanish colony, Central America had few resources to offer: a small supply of gold and silver; vegetable dyes; and cacao, the beans of which are used to make chocolate. It was not until the mid-1800s, after Central America won its independence from Spain, that its exports began to enter world markets.

In the 1850s, planters began to cultivate coffee in El Salvador. It was so successful that by 1870 coffee had replaced the dye *indigo* as the nation's major export. Several other Central American countries quickly entered the coffee market, too.

Banana plantations, established in the Caribbean lowlands around 1900, hoped for the same success. Eventually, coffee and bananas became the two most important exports of all Central American countries, earning them the nicknames "banana republics" or "coffee republics." Investors built railroads and ports to handle these exports. To bring in the harvests, hundreds of thousands of Indians and poor *mestizos* were hired every season, only to be thrown out of work a few months later. Blacks from Caribbean islands also found work on plantations.

Coffee and bananas continued to be the two main exports of Central America until well after World War II. When prices were high, the countries growing them prospered. When prices were low, however, hundreds of thousands of workers suffered.

Poor farmers make up nearly three-quarters of all rural inhabitants in Central America today. Although farming is becoming less important economically, farmers continue to make a major contribution to the welfare of each nation. They produce mostly corn, beans, and squash, which make up a large part of people's diets. Depending on the climate, *subsistence* farmers may also produce grains, fruits, vegetables, and meat products for the commercial market. Moreover, the subsistence farmer is critically important as a source of cheap labor during the seasonal harvests of coffee, sugar, and cotton.

Economic Growth Since the 1950s

Trying to solidify their economies, some Central America countries began exporting cotton in the 1950s. The United States *embargo* of sugar from Cuba after 1959 led to a major increase in the export of Central American sugar during the 1960s. In the 1970s, beef became a major export, needed to meet the needs of the

U.S. fast-food industry. All of these products came from coastal lowlands in Panama, Costa Rica, Nicaragua, and Guatemala.

Since the 1950s, economic growth in Central America has brought improvement in transportation. New roads and highways began crisscrossing the land during a transportation boom in the 1960s. The Inter-American Highway extends nearly all the way through the isthmus. In 1960, Central America began to attract foreign investment by businesses and governments after the creation of the Central American Common Market (CACM).

Today, manufactured goods make up between one-quarter and one-third of the exports of the CACM. Most manufacturing takes place in or near cities. About one-half of all manufacturing deals with food processing, beverages, tobacco, textiles, shoes, and clothing. Producing chemicals and pharmaceuticals, refining petroleum, making cement, and processing paper and wood products contribute another one-quarter. Other types of manufacturing vary. Most Central American countries trade manufactured goods with each other, which does not bring in large enough profits for economic development.

Economic growth continued for the countries of Central America during the 1960s and early 1970s, until several setbacks occurred. Beginning in the mid-1970s, prices for imported oil rose. At the same time, prices for Central American exports

Major Exports

- Belize: sugar cane, clothing, fish, bananas, wood and molasses.
- Costa Rica: bananas, pineapples, coffee, melons, ornamental plants, sugar, seafood, electronic components and medical equipment.
- El Salvador: offshore assembly exports, coffee, sugar, shrimp, textiles, chemicals, and electricity.
- Guatemala: coffee, sugar, petroleum, clothing, bananas, fruits and vegetables, and cardamum.
- Honduras: coffee, shrimp, bananas, gold, palm oil, fruit, lobster, and lumber.
- Nicaragua: coffee, shrimp, lobster, beef, sugar, gold, peanuts and tobacco.
- Panama: bananas, shrimp, sugar, coffee, and clothing.

Source: CIA World Factbook 2008.

These whitewater rafters are visiting Cocos Island in Costa Rica. Many people from all over the world are drawn to Central America because of the region's unspoiled natural beauty. Tourism is the top source of revenue for Costa Rica. Ecotourism—responsible travel that contributes to conserving natural environments—is growing more popular among visitors to Central America.

dropped. These nations had borrowed billions of dollars at high interest rates to finance their development. In the early 1980s, they began to have trouble paying back the loans. Civil wars, border disputes, and political tensions throughout Central America made the economic situation much worse.

In June 1990, President George Bush proposed encouraging the growth of free-market economies in Central America, first by canceling part of their debt to the United States; and second, by promising to work towards establishing a *free trade* zone throughout North, Central, and South America. A free trade zone lowers the trade restrictions between countries. The passage of the North American Free Trade Agreement (NAFTA) in 1993, however, tended to favor Mexico as the economic powerhouse in the region, giving it an overwhelming competitive advantage over Central American countries. In 2006, El Salvador, Honduras, Nicaragua, and Guatemala officially implemented the Central American Free Trade Act (CAFTA) with the United States. Results have been mixed, causing uncertainty in Costa Rica about whether to ratify CAFTA.

Environmental Crisis Looms

Despite the recent economic growth, Central America remains one of the poorest regions on earth. Nevertheless, the population of Central America is sky-rocketing. It has more than tripled since the early 1900s. This population explosion has led to widespread unemployment and contributed to environmental problems.

Rural forests are cut down and burned for firewood or used in the production of paper, and large tracts of land are cleared for agriculture. These activities have led to large-scale erosion and soil loss, leaving many areas open to flash floods and mudslides. The result of abusing the land was tragically shown in 1998, when Hurricane Mitch—the region's most violent storm in over 200 years—hit large parts of Central America. Floods and mudslides killed thousands of people and caused billions of dollars in damages.

In addition, pollution from cars, industry, and power generation is a major problem in several areas. Like much of Latin America, Central America's cities experienced large population growth throughout the 1990s. This growth has, in most cases, resulted in an increase in the number of motor vehicles, leading to more urban air pollution. The number of motor vehicles on roads has increased up to 16 percent each year. It is estimated that nearly 70 percent of all urban air pollution in the Central American region is caused by cars, trucks, buses, and motor-bikes.

Fortunately, the region benefits from financial help from numerous outside organizations, such as the World Bank, the U.S. Agency for International Development (USAID), and the U.S. government. In 1999, for example, the Clinton administration committed to a second five-year, $25-million program to support environmental protection programs in Central America. Still, Central Americans, with the help of the rest of the world, must work hard if they are to overcome such environmental losses.

(Opposite) A group of children look at a display showing a map of Costa Rica in the Children's Museum in San José. Most of the people of Costa Rica are *mestizo*—of mixed Amerindian and European descent. (Right) A Mayan youngster holds her baby sister. Descendants of the Maya and other Amerindian groups make up about 20 percent of Central America's population today.

4 The People of Central America

THERE ARE 41 MILLION people in Central America. One-fifth of this total are Amerindians. *Mestizos*—people of mixed white and Indian heritage—make up one-half of the population. Spanish is the official language of all the Central American countries except Belize, where the official language is English. Many Indians in Guatemala speak their own tribal languages.

A Change in Empires

When the Europeans arrived in the New World in 1492, Central America had a population of about 5 million Amerindians. Most of these lived in areas controlled by the Maya. However, after A.D. 900, the power of the Maya had begun to decline. Perhaps the area they tried to control was too large, causing shortages of food and a breakdown of their society.

31

Whatever the cause, the result was that Spanish forces succeeded in conquering key areas of Central America. No more than 10,000 or 15,000 Europeans swept through Central America between the early 1500s and 1600. Meeting no large-scale Amerindian resistance, small armies brought large areas under their control. Still, the Maya held out longer against the Spanish than the Aztecs of Mexico did or the Incas of Peru.

This upheaval nearly destroyed the Amerindians of Central America. Millions died of starvation or foreign diseases—measles, smallpox, and malaria—against which the Indians had no immunity. Others lived in slavery. A sizable number of Mayans went to northern Guatemala, establishing the city of Tayasal as a place of refuge. There they maintained their independence until 1697.

The remaining Amerindians still living in Spanish-controlled territory gathered into villages and towns. Many converted to Roman Catholicism, though some continued to practice traditional rituals. They learned to raise sheep, pigs, horses, and cows—strange animals unknown to them before the Spanish arrived. They also learned to use metal tools and they were taught how to craft products of fiber, clay, wood, leather, and metal. This kind of labor was needed by the Spanish, who wanted to bring European ways to the New World. A new group of people arose—the *mestizo* (often called the *ladino* in Guatemala), a racial group made up of mixed white and Indian blood.

Religions

- Belize: Roman Catholic, 49.6 percent; Protestant, 27 percent; none, 9.4 percent; other: 14 percent.
- Costa Rica: Roman Catholic, 76.3 percent; Protestant, approximately 14 percent; other, 9.7 percent.
- El Salvador: Roman Catholic, 83 percent; Protestant, 17 percent.
- Guatemala: Roman Catholic, 60 percent; Protestant, 10 percent, traditional Mayan beliefs, 30 percent.
- Honduras: Roman Catholic, 97 percent; Protestant minority, 3 percent.
- Nicaragua: Roman Catholic, 72.97 percent; Protestant, 27.1 percent.
- Panama: Roman Catholic, 85 percent; Protestant, 15 percent.

A small number of blacks were introduced into colonial Central America by the Spanish and the English during the 16th and 17th centuries. After 1850, several hundred thousand blacks emigrated from the Caribbean islands, drawn by the need for labor for building the Panama Canal and railroads, and for establishing banana plantations on the Caribbean coast. Today, blacks are a large part of the population along the Caribbean coast of Central America.

A Population Explosion

The population of Central America did not return to 5 million until 1930. By then, however, Amerindians had become a minority. After this the population increased rapidly, growing to 12 million by 1950 and over 41 million by 2007. This rapid rate of growth increased *population density*, particularly in Guatemala and El Salvador, where 58 percent all Central Americans live. The most crowded country in Central America is El Salvador. In 1900, 800,000 people lived within its borders. The number doubled to 1.6 million by 1940. Today the total is about 7.1 million. Currently, El Salvador's population density is 882 persons per square mile (337 per sq. km), and the population is growing at an estimated rate of 1.68 percent.

The steady increase in Central America's population forced people off the land and into the cities. Between 1970 and 1985, the proportion of the population living in cities increased from one-third to one-half. *Slums* are a major problem in many urban areas. Despite the stream of people into the cities, those who remain in rural areas feel the squeeze of too many people trying to raise food on too little land. Rural poverty is a fact of life in nearly every Central American country.

Country by Country

Belize is the most sparsely populated nation in Central America, with a population of 300,000. Slightly more than half of the people live in rural areas. About one-fourth live in Belize City, the principal port, commercial center, and former capital. Most Belizeans are of multiracial descent. Many Belizeans, more than one-third, are black or of partly black ancestry. Six languages are commonly spoken in the various towns and villages.

The 4.2 million Costa Ricans are the most racially alike of any Central Americans. They are 94 percent *mestizos* (of mixed white and American Indian descent); 3 percent black; 1 percent American Indian; 1 percent Chinese; and 1 percent belonging to other racial groups. The lighter complexion of Old World settlers can be seen everywhere. In fact "whiteness," and the lack of a strong surviving Indian culture, creates part of Costa Ricans' sense of national identity. They call themselves *ticos*, which probably comes from a saying in Spanish colonial days, "We are all *hermanitos* (little brothers)."

El Salvador's population numbers about 7.1 million. Almost 90 percent are of mixed Indian and Spanish descent. Nine percent are white. Only about 1 percent is Amerindian, and very few still observe Amerindian customs and traditions. Nearly all Salvadorans speak Spanish, and most are Roman Catholic, although Protestant groups are growing. About 1.7 million people live in the capital, San Salvador, but almost half of El Salvador's population lives in the countryside.

Guatemala's population of 13 million is divided into two main ethnic groups—the Indians, who account for 44 percent of the population, and the Ladinos, which is a term used to define all non-Indians, such as *mestizos* (mixed Indian and Spanish ancestry), **mulattoes**, black Africans, and Europeans. Ladinos account for 56 percent of the population. Other Ladino minorities include Black Caribs or Morenos, Asians, Lebanese, and Syrians.

About 90 percent of Honduras's population of 7.6 million is *mestizo*. Most of the Indians are Lenca and are now found in the southwest, near the Guatemala border, close to the most important Indian centers of the Mayan period. More than 100 years ago, immigrants from Caribbean islands settled in the Caribbean Lowlands and the Bay Islands. These people, known as the Garifuna, or Black

Caribs, live in 44 coastal villages. Then, in the 1970s and 1980s, a new population—approximately 50,000 refugees—arrived in Honduras to escape the civil unrest in surrounding countries. Most are housed by the United Nations in camps near the borders, but numerous uncounted illegal refugees are scattered throughout the country.

Most of the 5.8 million Nicaraguans are *mestizos*. About 17 percent of the population is white, 9 percent black, and 5 percent of the population is Amerindians. Differences in culture, language, and appearance create friction between *mestizos* of the Central Highlands and Pacific Lowlands and non-*mestizo* minorities of the east or Caribbean Lowlands. In the eastern half of Nicaragua, far away from the decision-making centers of power on the other side of the mountains, Amerindians and Creoles prefer to remain apart from the Spanish-speaking whites and *mestizos* in language, customs, and lifestyles.

Panama's importance as a crossroads between two oceans mixed people from all over the world. Except for Belize, the 3.3 million people of Panama are racially more diverse than the rest of Central America. Seventy percent of Panamanians are *mestizo*; 14 percent are mixed Amerindian, Asian, and African; 10 percent are white; and 6 percent are Amerindian. Many people have ancestors who were African slaves. The *mestizo* and mixed populations are concentrated within the Canal Zone and along the Pacific lowlands of western Panama. Spanish is the official language, although English and Indian dialects are also spoken. The Amerindians are located in isolated highland pockets and along the Caribbean shoreline east of the Canal Zone. There are three major Indian groups: the Kunas on the San Blas Islands off the Caribbean coast, the Emberá in the province of Darién, and the Guaymies in the Chiriquí, Bocas del Toro, and Veraguas provinces.

It's likely that problems associated with rapid population growth will continue to plague Central America, unfortunately. The annual population growth rate is 1.8 percent.

(Opposite) A Guatemalan girl and her mother pause in front of their simple house in the El Petén district of Guatemala. The home is constructed of sticks and straw. A large percentage of the people of Central America live in poverty. (Right) A Costa Rican craftsman carefully paints the wheel of a decorative oxcart. The people of Costa Rica, like others of Central America, are known for their crafts.

5 The Communities and Cultures of Central America

CENTRAL AMERICA IS home to various African, Native American, and European cultures, widely sharing the Spanish language and the Catholic faith. On the other hand, not everyone speaks Spanish, either. Thousands of Central Americans prefer to speak English or Amerindian languages.

The Family is Central

The family is central to Central American daily life and society. Family ties contribute to people's identity, and relatives help one another in business. According to custom, families—usually including grandparents, aunts, uncles, and cousins—tend to be large and to live together under one roof. Married children who set up their own households usually do so in the same village or neighborhood as their parents. Some family members add to the household income by learning crafts: woodcarving (notably wooden instruments), basketry, embroidery and textile arts, leather craft, and ceramics. These are sold on market days or in tourist areas.

Central Americans usually marry in religious ceremonies, but civil marriages performed by a judge are common, too. Many couples sometimes live together until they can afford a religious ceremony and a wedding celebration. Close, trusted friends are often brought into family circles by being designated *compadres* ("godparents"), an honor—and a responsibility—that is often given at marriages and baptisms.

Increasingly, though, common-law marriages (without a church ceremony or a license) occur among the poor. More than half of all children are born out of wedlock. Some parents who are unable to care for their children even abandon them. El Salvador's orphanages—crowded during the civil war—are still bleak and underfunded.

The Influence of Religion

The Roman Catholic religion is an important part of the region's Spanish heritage. On average, about three-quarters of the population is Roman Catholic. The remaining are either Protestant, members of other faiths, or nonbelievers. Some country people, especially Amerindians, have blended the Catholic faith with practices of Amerindian faiths. They attend the Catholic mass, for instance, but bring baskets of corn to church to be blessed by the priest, just as their Mayan ancestors offered corn and other gifts to their gods. They sometimes pray to the ancient gods, too, for a good harvest, as well as to the Christian saints for blessings.

Protestant sects have won thousands of converts in recent years. The Assemblies of God, the Seventh Day Adventists, the Church of God, and a few Pentecostal groups are all attracting increasing numbers of worshippers. Baptists, too, are active in countries such as El Salvador with programs to help those in need of health care, housing, and food.

In some way, religion has a place in almost every Central American person's life. Some rural areas do not have churches, and traveling priests visit them only three or four times each year. In such villages, the priest's arrival signals a flurry of baptisms, confirmations, marriages, and funeral services. Missionary work by Protestant groups attracts hundreds to meetings and prayer services.

Mayan Separateness

Mayan beliefs and traditional ways have lasted for centuries, primarily in Guatemala, because the Indians tried to seal themselves off from outside interference. Indian communities deliberately kept their ways of life secret. They tried to resolve their own problems rather than turn them over to colonial authorities. Unfortunately, the Indians' differences also gave their colonial masters excuses to abuse them as outsiders. Most native communities still keep themselves apart from Europeans.

One of the main rallying points for present-day Mayan culture is demanding respect for their languages. Although Spanish is the most widely spoken language, there are also more than 20 native languages used throughout Guatemala. In 1990, the Guatemalan government legally recognized the Academy of Mayan Languages. Soon, all teachers in Mayan areas will be *bilingual*, teaching Mayan children in their native tongue as well as in Spanish.

National Holidays

Nearly all Central American countries celebrate public holidays on these dates. In addition, most have a Mother's Day at various times of the year.

- January 1—New Year's Day.
- March/April—Holy Thursday/Good Friday/Easter Sunday.
- May 1—Labor Day.
- September 15—Independence Day.
- October 12—Columbus Day.
- November 1, 2—All Saints' Day/Day of the Dead.
- December 24—Christmas Eve.
- December 25—Christmas Day.
- December 31—New Year's Eve.

Clothing is another way Mayan Guatemalans distinguish themselves. Although Mayan men usually dress in western clothing—except in a few parts of the country—Mayan women still tend to wear a long *corte* (skirt) and a *huipil* (blouse). On festival days, the colorful and rich designs of embroidered tunics, capes, and skirts date back to before colonial times. There are 23 different attires for men and women, depending on the native group and region. Details of hand-made garments and designs identify the wearer's group and village. Designs and colors of clothing can have religious, symbolic, or magical meanings, too.

Clothing Expresses Culture

Wealthy and middle-class city dwellers dress like North Americans and Europeans—dresses for the women and suits for the men. Women rarely wear pants, but jeans are popular among young men and women alike. In the country-side, however, older ways of dressing endure. Traditional costumes are often seen at festivals, too.

A Panamanian woman shows off her *pollera*. It is made with row after row of finely tucked muslin. Over this goes a full, ankle-length skirt of wide bands, separated by lace whose pattern is the same as that embroidered or appliquéd on the white of the *pollera*. The blouse has a deep, embroidered or appliquéd band, edged in lace and gathered onto a neckband, through which is woven yarn ending, front and back, in big pompoms. It's not unusual for women to work for months to create a *pollera*.

In the countryside in El Salvador, for example, men wear hats to keep the sun off, usually large hats woven of palm leaves. Country women wear ankle-length skirts and loose blouses, most often in dark colors. They often cover their heads with shawls or scarves if a stranger approaches. Most Salvadorans only have two or three changes of clothes, including one for special occasions.

During festivals, Panama's folklore is fully expressed in its traditional dances, its colorful *pollera*, the national costume, and *templeques* (hair ornaments) worn by women. Embroidered, long-sleeved shirts, calf-high trousers, and a straw *montuno* hat is the national costume worn by men.

Food and Drink

Many dishes in Central America are based on corn, as corn has a deep cultural meaning for these countries. Quetzalcoatl, a mythical hero who guided the Amerindians, put a grain of corn on the lips of the first man and woman, enabling them to think and work. Today, corn is the primary ingredient used in main dishes, drinks, desserts, and other refreshments. Cassava (yuca), beans, and chili pepper are also widely used as ingredients in different dishes.

For instance, a typical meal in Nicaragua consists of eggs or meat, beans and rice, salad (cabbage and tomatoes), tortillas, and fruit in season. Food is usually scooped up in tortillas instead of using knives and forks. Most common of all Nicaraguan foods is *gallo pinto*, a blend of rice and beans. Other traditional dishes include *bajo*, a mix of beef, green and ripe plantains, and cassava, and *vigorón*— cassava served with fried pork skins and coleslaw. Street vendors sell drinks such as *tiste*, made from cacao and corn, and *posol con leche*, a corn-and-milk drink. Roasted corn on the cob is also sold on the streets.

In Honduran households, the meals are based around beans, rice, tortillas, fried bananas, meat, potatoes, cream, and cheese. Celebrations bring out specialty dishes, such as tamales and *yucca con chicharrón* (fried cassava and pork). There are

A mixture of fried meat, peppers, and cornmeal dough is placed inside a cornhusk to make a *tamale*—a popular dish in Central America.

also many comidas típicas (typical foods) special to various regions of the country, including *sopa de hombre* (man's soup) and other seafood dishes in the south; *queso con chile* (cheese with chili peppers) in the west; and *cazabe* (mashed cassava) among Garifuna or Black Caribs in the Caribbean Lowlands.

Music—the Marimba

The most popular instrument in many parts of Central America is the marimba, a xylophone made of wood. Marimbas vary greatly in size, from smaller ones played by one or two players, up to instruments played by 6 or 8 players at once. It originated in pre-Columbian Mexico and Guatemala, and was adopted as El Salvador's national instrument during the 20th century. The first mention in history of the marimba as a native instrument appears in the *Compendium of the History of Guatemala*, written by the Spanish historian Juan Domingo Juarros. He describes marimba musicians playing at the opening of the cathedral in Antigua in 1806. The origins of the marimba also appear in an ancient Mayan manuscript, where an Indian musician plays a type of marimba made from a log. Today, marimba orchestras featuring trumpets, saxophones, banjos, and percussion instruments play in cities for ballroom parties and important public celebrations.

Certain areas of Central America are known for traditional Indian music. In Costa Rica, for example, the heartland of traditional Indian music and dancing is the province of Guanacaste. Here, instruments used before Columbus, such as the *chirimia* (oboe) and *quijongo* (a single-string bow with gourd resonator), are still used for Chorotega tribal dances. In addition, the Borucas still perform their "Danza de los Diablitos," and the Talamancas their "Danza de los Huelos." Spanish-influenced dances are usually about enchanted lovers. They are mostly based on the Spanish *paseo*, with women in white blouses and colorful skirts circled by men in white suits and cowboy hats.

On the Caribbean coast, music is Afro-Caribbean in spirit and rhythm. African-derived marimba music of Costa Rica is heard alongside the guitar, a popular instrument, especially as an accompaniment to folk dances such as the "Punto Guanacaste," a stomping dance for couples, officially decreed as the national dance. Drums and banjos accompany a dance in which each person holds one of many brightly colored ribbons tied to the top of a pole. As they dance, they braid the ribbons. Visitors can hear calypso and reggae, too, both of which are played throughout the Caribbean.

(Opposite) Hundreds of Roman Catholics carry the figure of Jesus Christ during a Palm Sunday procession in the town of Panchimalco, El Salvador. Religion is an important aspect of life in Central America, and a majority of the population is Catholic. (Right) Costumed musicians play a beautiful wooden marimba, a xylophone-like instrument that originated in Guatemala.

6 The Festivals of Central America

THE ROMAN CATHOLIC Church and its history play an important role in the lives of Central Americans. As a result, many holidays and festivals are rooted in Roman Catholic traditions and practices. Besides religious holidays, two other types of holidays are also celebrated in Central America. First, there are holidays that recall historic events. Second, there are holidays that celebrate, through music, food, and dance, the cultures of different peoples, such as the Maya, the Garifuna, and the Black Caribs.

Religious Holidays: Saints, Parades, and Church Services

El Salvador is mainly a Catholic nation, and its biggest holidays are religious in nature. El Salvador's most important national religious festival falls during the first week of August in honor of the Holy Savior of the World, "El Salvador," for whom the country is named. During this week, a wooden image of Jesus, carved in 1777, is paraded through the streets of San Salvador to the National Palace and the cathedral, after which a band plays the national anthem. People flock to the capital city to enjoy the colorful processions, a large *feria* (fair), carnival rides, fireworks, soccer matches, and homemade foods.

The festival also includes special sporting events: soccer matches, bicycle races, and boxing matches. Carnivals do a thriving business. A local official crowns the Queen of the August Fair. Artists create artworks on sidewalks out of dyed sawdust, similar to sand paintings made by southwestern Indians in North America.

As another example of the religious influence on Central American celebrations, in Costa Rica, nearly a month is dedicated to celebrating Christmas. Beginning in early December, homes and businesses put up *portales* (nativity scenes). Competition for the best *portal* runs through December 22. Special foods are prepared for family members and visitors, including coconut *melcochas* (candy), *chicha* (a heady brew made from corn), *tamales*, *rompope* (egg nog), and imported apples and grapes. Starting around December 15, carolers go from house to house and are treated to refreshments. At midnight on December 24, Catholic churches celebrate the *Misa de Gallo*—Mass of the Rooster. After the service, worshippers return home to prepare for a day of family events on Christmas.

Many towns in Central America have patron saints or saints whose lives or works have a special connection to the town. El Salvador and Nicaragua are good examples of religious celebrations of this kind.

In El Salvador, every town and city has its own patron saint, whose day is celebrated annually with a fiesta. The celebration helps keep local traditions alive. Fireworks and band concerts attract families. Children take a whack at piñatas, trying to break them. Piñatas are shaped like animals and made from cardboard, paste, and colored paper. They are filled with candy, which spills out when a

The colonial-era Catholic church La Merced in Antigua, Guatemala, is decorated with an elaborate *alfombra* (carpet) of colored sawdust and flowers during a celebration of *Semana Santa* (Holy Week) in Antigua.

lucky, blindfolded child shatters the toy with a bat.

Like El Salvador, each city in Nicaragua has its own patron saint, and some saints are shared between towns. Devout people offer gifts to saints in exchange for blessings, such as a healing, a good crop, or children. Part of the tradition of honoring a saint is holding a fiesta as well.

In Nicaragua, as in all Central American countries, fiestas are holidays of fun and excitement in villages, towns, and cities. A statue of the saint being honored is carried through the streets, signaling the start of traditional dances, plays, or rituals. Following behind the saint's image, people offer flower arrangements, and they "pay" for their blessings with little gold and silver objects and fruit bunches. As night falls, exploding firecrackers and fireworks add to the pleasure of entertainment by roving musicians, performing clowns, and speeches by local leaders.

Historical Celebrations: Reenactments and Ceremonies

Celebrations that recall historic events are quite popular in Central America, too. In Belize, for example, Baron Bliss Day honors the British nobleman who willed his fortune to Belize. A harbor regatta, or boat parade, is held in front of the lighthouse where the baron's grave is located. Later in the day, crowds cheer on horse and bicycle races. In a similar way, St. George's Caye Day in Belize commemorates a battle in 1798 when slaves, settlers, and British soldiers defeated the Spanish fleet. Carnivals, sporting activities, fire engine parades, and pop concerts lead up to the celebration.

In Costa Rica, the Fiesta of the Diablitos, held in the Indian village of Rey Curré, stages a fight between Indians (*diablitos*) and the Spanish (a bull). Colorful wooden masks and costumes create the scene. On April 11, Juan Santamaría Day in Costa Rica commemorates Costa Rica's national hero, the barefoot young soldier who gave his life in a dangerous mission against William Walker's troops in 1856. Weeklong celebrations feature marching bands, parades, concerts, and dances.

In Panama, a long-standing tradition—a weeklong Carnaval, which is similar to Mardi Gras in New Orleans—gradually blended with the opening of the Panama Canal. Celebrated since the early 1900s, Panama's Carnaval officially begins the fourth day before Ash Wednesday as a religious observance; however, many celebrations begin earlier. On the actual carnival days, most work comes to a complete stop, and the main streets of Panama City are filled with parades, floats, masks, costumes, and confetti.

Cultural Celebrations: Costumes, Dancing, and Food

Cultural celebrations in Central America emphasize what makes various groups special, either through their lifestyle or their values. In Guatemala, for example, folkloric festivals have grown out of the legends from the past. All traditional fiestas include folk dancing, the forms of which date back hundreds of years to the Spanish conquest in the 1500s and before. Some of these dances are rooted in traditions brought from Spain, which include Moorish and Iberian influences. Others spring from Mayan tradition; still others have African roots, brought to the Caribbean by slaves. During the first week of August in Guatemala, throughout the region of Cobán, the Kekchi Indians wear traditional costumes, prepare special delicacies, and perform folk dances such as the Paabanc.

On *Todos Santos* (All Saints' Day) on November 1, families decorate the graves of loved ones in the afternoon. In the small village of Santiago, located about 15 minutes from Antigua, townspeople gather to fly giant kites high in the sky. With messages tied to the tails, the kites are symbols of communicating with loved ones who have passed away. The Itzá Indians blend the Catholic observance of All Saints' Day with their own traditional practices of remembering ancestors. On the evening of November 2, they perform ceremonies around a few real skulls of their ancestors. Also on that night, the children of San Francisco go door to door wearing masks and asking for treats.

In Costa Rica, the *Fiesta de los Negritos* in December is another example of Central American Indians blending two cultures. Held in the Indian village of Boruca, an ancient Indian ceremony honoring the dead is combined with one honoring the Virgin of the Immaculate Conception. Extravagant costumes, music, and dancing delight participants and visitors alike.

Some cultural festivals in Central America are important because they acknowledge what the rhythm of life is like in Central America. In El Salvador, for example, some fairs and festivals center on the seasons of farming. There is a Sugar Cane Fair in the town of Cojutepeque in January. The Flower Fiesta takes place in Panchimalco in May, and the Straw Festival in Zacatecoluca takes place in November. In Nicaragua during festival times, people look forward to seeing traditional dances and skits performed to music at certain times of the year.

The Countries of Central America: Maps

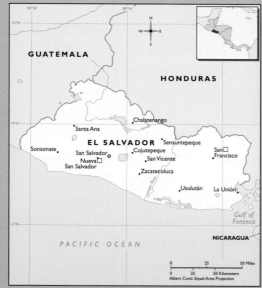

The Countries of Central America: Maps

Recipes

Honey Candy—Belize

(Serves 8 to 10)
1 pound honey
1/2 pound sugar
2 oz. butter

Directions:

1. Boil ingredients until a glob hardens when dropped in cold water.
2. Turn out boiled ingredients into shallow plates. Be careful, as this will be hot.
3. When cool enough to handle, twist or work into desired shapes.

Black Beans, Hearts of Palm, and Corn Salad—Costa Rica

(Serves 4)
1 16-oz. can black beans, rinsed and drained
1 10-oz. package frozen corn, thawed and drained
1 15-oz. jar of hearts of palm, drained and cut into 1/4-inch-thick rounds
2 large tomatoes, seeded and diced
1/2 red onion, minced
1/2 cup chopped fresh cilantro
1/4 cup olive oil
3 tablespoons fresh lime juice
1 teaspoon ground coriander

Directions:

Mix all ingredients in medium bowl. Season salad to taste with salt and pepper. (Salad can be prepared one day ahead). Cover and refrigerate.

Arroz Con Leche—El Salvador

(Serves 4)
1/2 cup rice
1 stick cinnamon
2 cups water
1-1/2 cups sugar
4 cups milk
2 eggs, lightly beaten
2 tablespoons raisins

Directions:

1. Cook the rice for 15 minutes. Then, rinse in cold water and put into a pot with 2 cups water and cinnamon.
2. Cook over a medium flame until all the liquid has been absorbed. Reduce the heat, and add the sugar and the milk. Cook until the rice is done.
3. Add the eggs to the rice. Bring to a boil, then transfer at once to a serving dish and decorate with raisins.

Frijoles Negros Volteados (Fried Black Bean Paste)—Guatemala

(Serves 4)
2 cups black bean puree (canned refried black beans)
1 tablespoon oil

Directions:

1. Heat oil over moderate heat in skillet.
2. Add bean puree, and mix well with wooden spoon. Stir until puree thickens and liquid evaporates.

3. Continue to stir until mix begins to come away from skillet dryly.

Serve warm with tortillas, farmer's cheese, sour cream, bread, or with all at once.

Coconut Bread—Honduras

(Serves 6 to 8)
1 pound shredded coconut
3 cups all-purpose flour
1 tablespoons baking powder
1/2 cup butter
1 cup sugar
2 eggs
2 teaspoon salt

Directions:
1. Preheat oven to 350° F.
2. Mix dry ingredients in a large bowl.
3. Beat eggs and add to dry ingredients. Add melted butter.
4. Mix ingredients together. Add a little milk if the batch seems dry.
5. Pour into two lightly greased loaf pans or two lightly greased pie dishes.
6. Bake for about 40-45 minutes or until toothpick comes out clean from the center.

Chocolate Bananas—Nicaragua

(Makes 16)
8 firm bananas (not too ripe)
2 small cans of chocolate syrup

16 Popsicle sticks
A knife
Wax paper

Directions:
1. Peel bananas and cut in half.
2. Stick a Popsicle stick into each banana, making sure it goes in straight.
3. Coat the bananas with chocolate syrup by dipping them into a tall glass filed with the syrup.
4. Place the bananas on wax paper over a plate or cookie sheet, and put the bananas into a freezer until frozen.

Ceviche De Garbanzos—Panama

(Makes approximately eight servings)
3 12-oz. cans of garbanzo beans or chickpeas
1/2 cup cider vinegar
1 cup olive oil
1 finely chopped onion
2 to 3 tablespoons fresh chopped parsley
2 teaspoons dried oregano leaves
3 cloves of garlic, finely minced
1 tablespoon ketchup
1 cup fresh or frozen corn
salt and cayenne pepper to taste

Directions:
1. Mix all ingredients in a large glass bowl, and cover with plastic wrap.
2. Let stand in the refrigerator overnight. Serve cold.

Glossary

Backwater—an isolated or backward place.

Bilingual—speaking two languages.

Biodiversity—biological diversity shown by a variety of plants and animals.

Embargo—a government restriction or restraint on commerce, especially an order that prohibits trade with a particular nation.

Free trade—trade based on the unrestricted exchange of goods, with tariffs (taxes) only used to create revenue, not keep out foreign goods.

Galleon—a heavy square-rigged sailing ship of the 15th to early 18th centuries used for war or commerce.

Geothermal—heat energy produced from the Earth.

Guerrilla—a person who is part of an irregular army and uses tactics of sabotage.

Hieroglyph—a symbolic figure or character usually carved into stone.

Indigo—a blue dye made from plants.

Isthmus—a narrow strip of land connecting two larger land areas.

Left wing—favoring policies that are Communistic or Socialistic.

Magnitude—great size or amount.

Mulatto—a person of mixed black and white ancestry.

Nationalist—supporting a strong, independent government.

Outlier—a geological feature far away from the main body.

Pine barren—dense pine forest with little vegetation on the forest floor.

Poacher—a person who hunts illegally.

Population density—the number of people living in a specific area.

Richter scale—a scale for measuring the severity of earthquakes created by Charles F. Richter.

Rural—in the countryside.

Slum—a crowded city area with unsanitary, rundown housing.

Subsistence—the condition of being or managing to stay alive, especially when there is barely enough food or money for survival.

Tectonic—having to do with the structure of the earth's crust.

Trade wind—a wind blowing almost constantly in one direction, usually associated with the equator.

Viceroyalty—the administration that rules as the representative of the king or a sovereign.

Project and Report Ideas

Country Profile

Create a profile of one Central American country. Use the directions below to assemble an informative poster, suitable for display and comparison with other students in your class. Use the CIA World Factbook at www.cia.gov/cia/publications/factbook/ to find most of the information.

- Map: Carefully cut and paste the map labels where they belong on the map. Choose appropriate colors to enhance the map. You may want to show elevation, land use, climatic regions, or some other aspect, but be sure to add your symbols to the key. If this map is to be part of a series, you may want to be sure that each map in the series uses the same symbols to make comparisons easier.
- Flag: Use the flags on page 2 of this book, or locate a color picture of the flag in an almanac, encyclopedia, or atlas. Copy the map onto your poster and color it appropriately.
- Occupations: Make a pie graph showing the percentages of workers in agriculture, industry, and other occupations. Fill in the percentages of workers in each area. Color your graph green for agriculture, red for industry, and brown for others.
- Per Capita Income: Paste on or draw a $100 bill for every hundred dollars earned by an average person in this country each year.
- Communications: Cut and paste one figure for each person who must share a radio in this country. If there are three people per radio, for example, glue three figures by the radio. Do the same for televisions and telephones.

Reports

Write one-page, five-paragraph reports answering any of the following questions. Begin with a paragraph of introduction, then three paragraphs—each developing one main idea, followed by a concluding paragraph that summarizes your topic:

Who were conquistadors? What was their mission?

Are all rainforests the same all over the world? What characteristics do they have?

What is the history of the Richter scale used to measure earthquakes?

Who are poachers and how do they make money from stealing or killing animals?

What was Vasco Núñez de Balboa's march across Panama like in 1513?

Some countries in Central America have been nicknamed "banana republics." What does the term mean? Give examples.

Why did the French attempt at building a Panama canal fail?

Flashcards

Using the glossary in this book, create flashcards. Put the term on one side and the definition on the other. Practice with the cards in pairs. Then, choose two teams of three. Select a referee to say the term out loud, and then call on someone to give the definition. The referee's decision is final. Award points for each correct answer. You can also read the definition, and ask for the correct term instead!

Cross-Curricular Reports

- Using a picture of a Mayan temple, build a small-scale model or show what one of the famous sites looks like from the air. Using a picture again, re-create a Mayan glyph using model clay. A glyph is a symbolic figure or character usually carved into stone. Make it about the size of a textbook lying flat.
- In teams, assemble a list of the best Web sites for finding out about Central America. Devise a rating system. Include a one- or two-sentence summary about the site. Combine these sites into a comprehensive guide to Central America on the Internet for other classes to use.
- Make a poster showing where the trade winds are found near the equator. Explain to the class how they assisted sailing ships in reaching their destinations.
- Illustrate the way income and wealth are distributed in Guatemala as a pyramid. The U.S. State Department says, "The wealthiest 10 percent of the population receives almost one-half of all income; the top 20 percent receives two-thirds of all income. As a result, approximately 75 percent of the population lives in poverty, and two-thirds of that number live in extreme poverty."
- Write a report titled, "Five of the Strangest Animals Found in the Rainforests of Central America."
- Write a one-page book review of any one of the following books:
    Ada, Alma Flor. *The Gold Coin*. New York: Aladdin, 1994.
    Alexander, Lloyd. *The El Dorado Adventure.* New York: E. P. Dutton, 1987.
    Defoe, Daniel. *A General History of Pyrates.* (Manuel Schonhorn, ed.) New York: Dover, 1999.
    Moeri, Louise. *The Forty-Third War.* Boston: Houghton Mifflin, 1989.
    Taylor, Theodore. *The Cay.* New York: Avon Books, 1969.

Chronology

10,000 B.C.	Amerindian communities dot the landscape of present-day Costa Rica.
1500 B.C– **A.D. 1200**	The Mayan civilization grows and flourishes in the region that will become Belize, Honduras, and Guatemala.
1100	Pipil Amerindians populate the region of El Salvador.
1400s	Chorotegas, or "Fleeing People," arrive from southern Mexico in Costa Rica, bringing with them a highly developed civilization.
1501	The Spanish adventurer Rodrigo de Bastidas, sailing from Venezuela, arrives in the region of Panama, searching for gold.
1502	Christopher Columbus sails along the western coast of Central America, scouting it for resources and mapping the coastline.
1513	Vasco Núñez de Balboa marches from the Atlantic to the Pacific, proving that crossing the Isthmus of Panama is the shortest route between the oceans.
1520s	Spanish conquistadors and settlers filter into Honduras.
1523	Spanish Captain Pedro de Alvarado conquers Guatemala for the king of Spain.
1525	Alvarado defeats the tribes of El Salvador, bringing the area under Spanish rule.
1570	The Spanish establish an administrative center, the Audiencia of Guatemala, which governs all of Central America except Panama.
1638	A band of shipwrecked English sailors land on the shore of Belize.
Late 1600s	Puritans and English pirates settle the coast of Belize.
1821	Central American countries declare independence from Spanish rule.
1836	Britain claims the right to administer Belize (then called British Honduras).
1880–1890	A French company under Ferdinand de Lesseps attempts unsuccessfully to construct a sea-level canal on the site of the present-day Panama Canal.
1903	Panama proclaims its independence from Colombia and concludes the Hay-Bunau Varilla Treaty with the United States.

1914	The United States completes the existing 50-mile (83 km) Panama Canal.
1948	All the Central American states except Belize join with other Latin American countries and the United States to form the Organization of American States (OAS).
1960–96	Civil war in Guatemala leaves 200,000 dead.
1964	Anti-United States riots over control of the Panama Canal result in the deaths of four U.S. Marines and more than 20 Panamanians.
1969	El Salvador and Honduras fight the 100-hour Soccer War over border disputes.
1979–92	Civil war in El Salvador leaves 75,000 dead.
1981	The United States ends aid to Nicaragua after finding evidence that Nicaragua, Cuba, and the Soviet Union are supplying arms to rebels in El Salvador; Belize attains full independence from Britain, although it will remain part of the British Commonwealth.
1980s	Honduran refugee camps serve as military training grounds for the Contras, U.S.–aided troops fighting Communist-supported governments throughout Central America.
1986	The U.S. Congress announces the Reagan administration has been providing military aid to the Contras; the supplies were purchased with funds diverted from the sale of U.S. arms to Iran; the covert operation becomes known as the Iran-Contra Affair.
1987	Costa Rican president Oscar Arias Sánchez receives the Nobel Peace Prize for his efforts in leading five Central American presidents to sign his peace plan in Guatemala City.
1988	The Sandinista rebels of Nicaragua and the U.S.-backed Contras begin a cease-fire and are parties to a peace plan.
1989	President George Bush orders the U.S. military into Panama to capture dictator General Manuel Noriega for drug trafficking and endangering U.S. interests in the Canal Zone.
1998	Hurricane Mitch strikes Central America, killing hundreds of people.
1999	The United States turns over control of the Panama Canal to Panama.
2005	Over 250 people die in landslides, floods, and an earthquake throughout Central America.
2009	Work continues on a controversial project to widen the Panama Canal.

Further Reading/Internet Resources

Booth, John A., et al. *Understanding Central America: Global Forces, Rebellion, and Change*. Boulder, Colo.: Westview Press, 2005.

Evans, Susan Toby. *Ancient Mexico and Central America: Archaeology and Culture History*. New York: Thames and Hudson, 2008.

Foster, Lynn V. *A Brief History of Central America*. New York: Checkmark Books, 2007.

Henderson, James D., et al, editors. *A Reference Guide to Latin American History*. Armonk, N.Y.: M.E. Sharpe, 2000.

MacLeod, Murdo J. *Spanish Central America: A Socioeconomic History, 1520–1720*. Austin: University of Texas Press, 2007.

Parker, Matthew. *Panama Fever: The Epic Story of One of the Greatest Human Achievements of All Time—the Building of the Panama Canal*. New York: Doubleday, 2008.

Pearcy, Thomas L. *The History of Central America*. London: Palgrave Macmillan, 2006.

History and Politics

http://www.centralamericadaily.com/
http://www.latinworld.com/centro/
http://www.hartford-hwp.com/archives/47/
http://www.politicalresources.net/c_amer.htm
http://www.ticotimes.net/

Visiting Central America

http://www.centramerica.com/
http://regional.searchbeat.com/centralamerica.htm
http://www.lonelyplanet.com/destinations/

Belize Tourism Board
New Central Bank Building, Level 2
Gabourel Lane
P.O. Box 325
Belize City, Belize
Telephone: 011-501-2-31913
Toll-Free: 1-800-624-0686
E-mail: info@travelbelize.org
Internet: http://www.travelbelize.org

Costa Rica—Instituto Costarricense de Turismo
Apartado 777-1000
San Jose, Costa Rica
Telephone: (506) 222-1090
       or 223-1733, ext. 277
Toll-free U.S. number: 1-800-327-7033
Fax: (506) 223-5452 or 555-4997
Internet: http://www.tourism-costarica.com

Embassy of the Republic of El Salvador
Ambassador Rene Antonio Leon Rodriguez
2308 California Street NW
Washington, D.C. 20008
Telephone: (202) 265-9671

Guatemala Human Rights Commission/USA
3321 12th Street NE
Washington, DC 20017
Telephone: (202) 529-6599
E-mail: ghrc-usa@ghrc-usa.org
Internet: http://www.ghrc-usa.org

Honduras Institute of Tourism
2100 Ponce de Leon Blvd, Suite 1175
Coral Gables, FL 33134
Telephone: (305) 461-1601

Embassy of Nicaragua
1627 New Hampshire Avenue NW
Washington, D.C. 20009
Telephone: (202) 939-6570

**American Chamber of Commerce
and Industry in Panama**
Estafeta Balboa
Apartado 168
Panama, Republica de Panama
Telephone: (507) 269-3881
       or (507) 223-3508
E-mail: amcham@pan.gbm.net

Index

Page

Contributors

Senior Consulting Editor **James D. Henderson** is professor of international studies at Coastal Carolina University. He is the author of *Conservative Thought in Twentieth Century Latin America: The Ideals of Laureano Gómez* (1988; Spanish edition *Las ideas de Laureano Gómez* published in 1985); *When Colombia Bled: A History of the Violence in Tolima* (1985; Spanish edition *Cuando Colombia se desangró, una historia de la Violencia en metrópoli y provincia*, 1984); and co-author of *A Reference Guide to Latin American History* (2000) and *Ten Notable Women of Latin America* (1978).

   Mr. Henderson earned a bachelors degree in history from Centenary College of Louisiana, and a masters degree in history from the University of Arizona. He then spent three years in the Peace Corps, serving in Colombia, before earning his doctorate in Latin American history in 1972 at Texas Christian University.

Charles J. Shields, the author of all eight books in the DISCOVERING CENTRAL AMERICA series, lives in Homewood, a suburb of Chicago, with his wife Guadalupe, an elementary-school principal. He has a degree in history from the University of Illinois in Urbana-Champaign, and was chairman of the English department and the guidance department at Homewood-Flossmoor High School in Flossmoor, Illinois.